Former Arizona Youth

NASA

To Col. Frank Borman,

commander of the first moon flight, who has said: "Exploration really is

the essence of the human spirit."

explore grand canyon

FELTON O. GAMBLE, *author and photographer*

THE HUMAN SPIRIT HAS CARRIED great explorers to Grand Canyon. Conquistador Cardenas, with Cortez' party from Mexico, in 1540 was the first non-Indian to see it. Missionary Garces, from San Xavier del Bac (near present-day Tucson), was next to reach the Canyon in 1776. He also explored Havasu Canyon. In 1869, Major Powell led the first river expedition.

To explore Grand Canyon is a thrilling experience. Be an explorer today. Take a field trip. Shoot pictures of the scene. Learn about nature. Hike the trails. Observe geology. Hear ranger talks and study museum exhibits. Make a trip to Havasu Falls. Ride the river rapids. Be aware to leave unchanged the natural environment.

Some will explore by reading this book. All will be rewarded by new knowledge of nature, geology, trail skills, the importance of ecology, and the wonder of all of earth's splendor that is the incredible Grand Canyon of the Colorado River in Arizona.

Book design and illustrations by Robert Jacobson

PUBLISHED BY NORTHLAND PRESS, FORT VALLEY ROAD, P. O. BOX N, FLAGSTAFF, ARIZONA. ONE DOLLAR. LIBRARY CONGRESS NO. 77-161511, SBN NO. 87358-072-9. COPYRIGHT 1971 BY FELTON O. GAMBLE.

*About nature and
a picture-taking tour of
South and North Rim scenes*

Aim Your camera

Mark Johnson had just taken a picture of the Battleship Formation in the Grand Canyon from the wall in front of Bright Angel Lodge when he noticed an auburn-haired girl about his age focusing her camera for a picture.

Mark quietly walked up to her and after she had snapped her picture said, "Hello, I'm Mark Johnson. Would you please pose as a model for me?"

The girl laughed. "But I'm not a model."

Mark laughed too and explained that he was trying to make a picture show about Grand Canyon to have at his school. "Everyone says the best way to give people an idea of the bigness of this canyon is to pose someone in the foreground of the picture. How about it?"

"All right. I'll let you take my picture if I can take yours."

"First, you have to tell me your name," Mark teased.

"Janice Cole, and everyone calls me Jan," was the answer.

"Good, Jan, let's go down the walk."

It was a short distance to the spot Mark thought would make a great picture, and, surprise! Jan stepped quickly to a safe place on the rock.

Mark said, "Say, this makes a mighty good picture with the beautiful formations of the Canyon for a background."

Jan looked and gasped, "It is beautiful!"

After Mark took her picture, he said, "Can you believe that it's eight miles across and those mountain formations below us are four times higher than the Empire State Building?"

"I would like to ride a mule down to the river hidden in the inner gorge and look up. Then I guess I'd know how deep it is."

"Why not? Maybe we can go together," Mark suggested.

"Maybe yes, maybe no," Jan laughed.

"Let's go up the walk and see if we can catch some more pictures," Mark suggested.

On the walk in front of the El Tovar Hotel they stopped at a place where a pipe mounted on the wall could be aimed like a spyglass. It pointed to canyon features, such as Indian Gardens and the Bright Angel Canyon which extends 18 miles to the north from the Colorado River.

As Mark leaned on the wall to take a picture of trails in the Canyon below them, Jan snapped a candid shot of Mark. He looked around and realized what she had done.

"That was a little tricky, Jan," he smiled, "but that's the way to get interesting pictures."

Mark took a Park Service leaflet out of his pocket. "This tells about a self-guided hike through the woods on the rim near here. I have a Nature Check List too. Would you like to see what we can find?"

"Sounds exciting," Jan replied. "I want to learn more about nature. I have been watching the birds and chipmunks in front of the Lodge."

As Mark led the way to the trail he said, "Here at Grand Canyon the air is so clear you can see for miles and we should get good photos. I come from a big city where man-made smog is terrible."

"I am glad people are trying to do something about all kinds of pollution," Jan commented. "In the town I come from we kids have a park clean-up project. We pick up litter in the grove and have cleared the banks of the stream. Now people enjoy the area and we hope it's better for wildlife too."

"The nature trail we are going to explore should show us something about ecology," Mark suggested. "How living things get along with each other in their environment is interesting."

Mark stopped to check his leaflet, "Here we are at the trail, we'll soon find out what's happening."

THE NATURE TRAIL

The nature trail leaflet told about 52 things to see, and each feature was marked on the trail by a number. Fourteen wild flowers were identified. Cactus and yucca plants, different kinds of trees, including a juniper four feet in diameter and 1,000 years old, and even birds, such as ravens that soar in the canyon, were listed.

Jan and Mark were fascinated, and Mark took many pictures including one of a heavenly blue Steller's Jay.

At the end of the trail, Jan declared, "I liked the secrets we discovered about nature."

"Like what?" Mark asked.

Jan replied, "Here are some about trees:"

1. Acorns are oak tree seeds. Deer, turkeys, and jays eat acorns.
2. Age of trees — a tree normally adds a ring of growth each year.
3. Bark scars from lighting may heal.
4. Bark beetles can kill trees. Usually birds control insects.
5. Making soil — dead trees decay and enrich the soil.

"Well, you have points on ecology as well as trees," Mark exclaimed.

"I have learned a lot," Jan said smiling.

As Jan and Mark walked back toward the hotel area, Mark told her about the replica of a Hopi Indian pueblo and a big dance circle platform near the rim.

INDIAN DANCES

"There'll be an Indian dance at 5:30," he concluded. Just then the loud, clear beat of Indian tom-toms sounded out, and Mark and Jan took off in a run. They could see the Indian boys entering the circle. These boys held several hoops in their hands, and as they danced to the tom-tom's beat they climbed in and out of the hoops, almost turning themselves inside out. Jan was fascinated by the colorful feathers and costumes worn by the Hopi Indians beating the tom-toms.

After the dance ended Mark asked one of the Indian dancers to pose for a picture with Jan. He agreed, and Jan held a hoop while Mark snapped another photo.

A new voice spoke out. "Jan, I've been looking for you." Jan spun around and there was her father.

Grand Canyon is a natural wonder of the world — from Desert View, S. Rim

"It's beautiful!" — from hotel area, S. Rim

"I want you to meet Mark Johnson, Dad," Jan said. "We have been having great fun taking pictures."

"Can you join us for dinner?" Mr. Cole invited after acknowledging the introduction.

"I'm sorry, but I'm expected back at the Lodge at six," Mark said regretfully.

"I hope we meet again," Jan said.

"I leave early tomorrow," Mark replied. "We'd better exchange home addresses now because I'd like to send you the picture I took of you." The addresses were quickly written.

"Goodbye, Jan. I'm glad we met," Mark said and took off on a run.

SCENES FROM EAST RIM DRIVE

The next morning Mark helped his mother and dad pack the car, and after breakfast they started to drive to the North Rim of the Canyon. On the East Rim drive, Mark had his dad stop so he could take pictures from the wall stop at Duck-on-Rock, Grandview Point, and at Desert View where Mark climbed to the top of the Watch Tower. From this vantage point he could take pictures of the Colorado River winding below for miles.

As they left the Park at Desert View, Dad remarked, "It's a 190-mile drive to reach the lodge on the other side."

"And they said it was only eight miles from rim to rim," Mark mused.

"No roads cross this big gully until we reach Navajo Bridge. Maybe you would like to try to jump it on a motorcycle," Dad suggested.

Mark laughed. "I heard about a fellow who thinks he can do just that, but he must be dreaming. Gravity would pull him down."

When they reached Navajo Bridge and looked down at the river, Mark was impressed by the big job it must have been to build this bridge. Farther north the road climbed higher and entered beautiful forests of spruce and pine.

As they turned a bend near the entrance to the Park, Mark spotted three deer crossing the road.

THE NORTH RIM IS WILD

"Dad, the forest seems different over here — and much wilder," Mark said.

"You're right," Dad agreed. "Remember that we are over a thousand feet higher than on the South Rim and some different trees grow here. Also, there are fewer visitors to this side. That could make a difference in the wilderness feeling."

Grand Canyon Lodge was located near spectacular Bright Angel Point (El. 8145). No sooner had Mark helped put the bags in their assigned cabin than he asked permission to look around until dinnertime. When granted, he took off like a jackrabbit with his camera slung over his shoulder.

Along a trail through the trees Mark noticed some boys and a girl ahead looking at a bush.

"Hi!" Mark greeted the group.

"Hello," was the reply.

One boy had a leaflet in his hand. "The number on the trail is 31, and the leaflet says this bush with red-colored branches is Mountain Mahogany."

Mark asked one of the boys where the trail led.

"All the way to the lookout on the end of Bright Angel Point."

As Mark left the group he thought that he would get a leaflet and do the nature trail later. Suddenly the path led out of the forest to a rocky prominence with a big drop

How can that big Duck on Rock balance?

"That looks like an Apollo Space Ship!" — Point Imperial, North Rim

on the sides and continued until it reached the very tip of the point where a railing made a safe lookout.

What a view! Nearby there were three spectacular temple formations which have been featured on a U.S. postage stamp. Mark stood alone at the point and studied the view. The South Rim was 11 airline miles away, and he was actually on the rim of Bright Angel Canyon. Far below he could see the Kaibab Trail that followed this canyon to the river. Someday he would make that hike.

Mark reached his cabin just about in time for dinner. The view from the dining room in the lodge was great, and Mark told his parents that he thought he could get some colorful sunset pictures after dinner.

"O.K.," his dad said, "but we go to bed as soon as the sun sets."

MORNING TRIP TO POINT IMPERIAL AND CAPE ROYAL

Next day Mark drove with his family to Point Imperial at the northeast lookout point. It was a delightful ride through the sweet-smelling forest. At the viewing area the forest came right down to the rim.

Cameraman Mark was busy as usual trying to find someone to pose. This time twin boys volunteered. They were wearing shorts and the skin on their backs was as tan as a berry. They looked fascinated by this earth wonderland. The Canyon is very wide here, and all kinds of shapes fill the gap. One formation, called Apollo Temple, looks just like an Apollo spaceship.

On the return trip, Dad said he thought there was time to drive to Cape Royal before lunch. There was another nature trail here, and Mark wished he could stay a month so he could do everything. They met a girl seasonal park ranger who was showing a girl where lightning had struck a tree. Of course Mark caught the picture. Further down the trail a wall of rock jutted out into the Canyon with a hole in it through which the river with a white-water rapids could be seen.

"This picture should make the show," Mark said excitedly.

Mark was surprised when Dad did not turn toward the village at the main road intersection.

THROUGH FOREST TO POINT SUBLIME

"We're going to take a wilderness road out to Point Sublime," Dad informed him.

"And I've brought a picnic lunch," Mother spoke up.

It was a wonderful 16-mile drive on a one-track road

through deep wild forest. Mark saw a flock of wild turkeys that flew away when the car approached. While eating lunch they watched a white-tailed Kaibab squirrel play around a tree trunk.

Finally, they reached Point Sublime. Mark took one look and exclaimed, "This has to be the greatest view in the Canyon!"

His dad was smiling and added, "They claim that you can look anywhere in an arc of 180 degrees and see a different sight."

Mark took a picture with an agave plant in the foreground and a terraced amphitheater of red rock in the background. Then he remarked that standing in the middle of the Canyon like this, it was too big to photograph. His mother laughed. Then it was time to start back.

That evening at dinner Mark asked if he could see the Park Service Ranger give his campfire show, "Dunes to Drifts."

"I should think you would be too tired," Dad replied.

"We leave tomorrow, so you can go to the show," Mother said.

Mark was thrilled to hear the Ranger tell about the six climate zones in this area and the different animals, birds, trees, shrubs, and flowers that grow in each zone. He showed pictures of sand dunes at the river where it is much warmer than at the rim where snowdrifts cover the cabins in winter. The pictures were great.

When Mark returned to his cabin and went to bed he could still smell the smoke of the piñon pine fire and he fell asleep planning his school show about his great visit to Grand Canyon.

PRIME CAMERA ACTION

1. Scenic views with people in foreground to show how big the Canyon is.
2. Muletrain party at the head of the trail and rounding bends.
3. Hikers with backpacks at the top of Bright Angel and Kaibab trails.
4. Deer along the road and in the forest.
5. Indian dancers in front of the Hopi House.
6. Campfire talk by ranger — flash picture.
7. View of the Canyon and the Colorado River.
8. Your friends and family standing on the edge of the rim.
9. Trail pictures taken on a hike or mule trip.

MORE THINGS TO EXPLORE

At the Canyon

1. Use Field Trip Check Lists on back pages of this book.
2. Go on ranger-guided and self-guided nature trail hikes.
3. Visit nature exhibits on South Rim at Visitor Center and Yavapai Museum; on North Rim at Information Center.

At Home

1. Get Grand Canyon pictures from magazines, travel folders, and postcards for a report.
2. Give a show at your school with color slides about the Canyon.
3. Locate trails, temples and towers, and places mentioned in this story on the topo map in this book.
4. Make a papier-mâché or clay model of the Grand Canyon from the map.

"Lightning scarred the bark"

Agave plants have grown at Point Sublime for centuries

*A geology field trip
down Kaibab Trail
to Phantom Ranch and
up Bright Angel Trail*

Hike From Rim to River

At the head of Kaibab Trail on the South Rim of Grand Canyon a group of young people gathered around a man checking a trail map. Each carried a gallon-size canteen and a knapsack, and notebooks were much in evidence. All were listening intently to the man explain how they would examine the formations and rocks they would find as they hiked down Kaibab Trail into the Canyon and across the Colorado River to Phantom Ranch.

"Even though we have talked about it many times, the big idea is to examine and identify the formations and the rocks, but while we enjoy all the natural wonders of this canyon and check them on our field lists, we will also preserve every stick, stone, weed, bush, flower, and tree so that others will be able to see the Canyon as it is. Remember that no one is allowed to remove any natural thing from the Canyon. Two million people visit it every year, and if each one of that two million took home a flower, very few seeds would be left to drop on the soil to grow more flowers. And if each one took home a rock from the accessible trails, they would soon be picked bare. The Canyon would lose the wilderness feeling that only comes from the pureness of untouched nature. Therefore, the specimens we will take home with us for our school exhibit will be the photographs made by Jack Sharper and the drawings of our two artists, Pam and Isabell."

A SCIENCE CLASS PLANS A FIELD TRIP

This big expedition had really started months before when Sue Green had asked a question in science class. She had been much interested by the stories of prehistoric dinosaurs and all the other mammals, birds, reptiles, and fish that had lived at different times, and she asked her teacher, Mr. Baker, "Do you know any place I can go to see fossil footprints of dinosaurs and maybe see some of the other fossils?"

Mr. Baker thought for a moment and then smiled broadly. "Sue, I've been thinking that I would like to take this whole class on a geology field trip to see the Grand Canyon, where the Colorado River has cut down through the surface of the earth to expose rocks from the different ages of our planet and fossils of things that lived in those ages. And we could make pictures of the fossils and rocks we find for a school exhibit, just as our astronauts take pictures of rocks on the moon."

The class went wild. Everyone wanted to go exploring in the Grand Canyon. When the noise quieted down, Sue asked, "Would you really take us if we could manage to organize a trip?"

"I certainly would," Mr. Baker affirmed.

And that was how it began. Coach Martin and his wife volunteered to go as counselors to take care of health and first aid, and a group of parents made arrangements for reservations and transportation.

Mr. Baker devoted several sessions of the science class to prepare the class for the field trip. The study of the earth is called geology, and the men who study it geologists. But there are many fields in geology. The men who study fossils are known as paleontologists, for example. One day he brought to class a large diagram.

GEOLOGIC CROSS SECTION AT KAIBAB TRAIL

"This is a geologic cross section of the Grand Canyon showing each rocky layer from rim to river. Pam and Isabell, you're the artists of the class. We'll enlarge this on the blackboard and color the layers just as we will see them in the Canyon. The colors come from the minerals in the rocks that make up each layer. Geologic eras and periods and thicknesses of the layers are bracketed at the side of the chart."

Another day was devoted to learning about the types of rock the hikers would find in the Canyon. Later in the week, Mr. Baker brought some rocks to class to be identified. This was the day the rockhounds shone. Bill Smith got his rock-testing kit from his locker and the class gathered around while he explained its contents.

"This is a magnifying glass I use to look for crystals, and this is a special tile to rub rocks on to get a streak of their true color. Here's a steel file and a piece of glass to test the hardness of the rock by scratching. This bottle contains vinegar to test for limestone and the other bottle is water to test for shale."

"Great!" exclaimed Mr. Baker. "We'll have you help us make up similar kits to take on our trip. Now, Bill, here's a rock. Let's put the kit to work." And he handed Bill a rock and passed out the other rocks for the rest of the class to examine.

"Well, Bill, what do you think?" Mr. Baker asked.

"It isn't heavy enough to contain copper or iron," Bill

Bill put a few drops of vinegar on the rock. The class gathered around to watch.

"Look at that!" Tom Hardin exclaimed. "It's bubbling. It's limestone. Where's it from?"

Mr. Baker grinned. "You just identified your first Grand Canyon rock. A friend of mine sent this Kaibab Limestone down to us from near Grand Canyon. See there on the chart that's the first layer we'll see as we start down the trail."

Ten days after school was out, the science class arrived at Grand Canyon early in the afternoon so there was time to visit the Yavapai Museum where they saw specimens of fossils from the rock formations and heard a girl ranger tell how the Canyon was formed. After a good night's sleep, "Baker's Rockhounds," as Coach Martin had named them, were at the top of Kaibab Trail ready to go down.

STARTING DOWN KAIBAB TRAIL

First, Mr. Baker reviewed the use of the topographic map published by the U.S. Geological Survey. This map was covered with wavy lines called "contour lines" or "contour intervals" that show the elevation and shape of the ground surface. These lines represent intervals of 80 feet and the elevations are given at 400-foot intervals. All elevations are given in relation to sea level, which is the starting point for measurement.

The boys and girls compared the map with the Canyon and discovered it was easy to see how the canyon walls are shaped and how the sides slope. The high points, like

Geologic cross section at Kaibab Trail

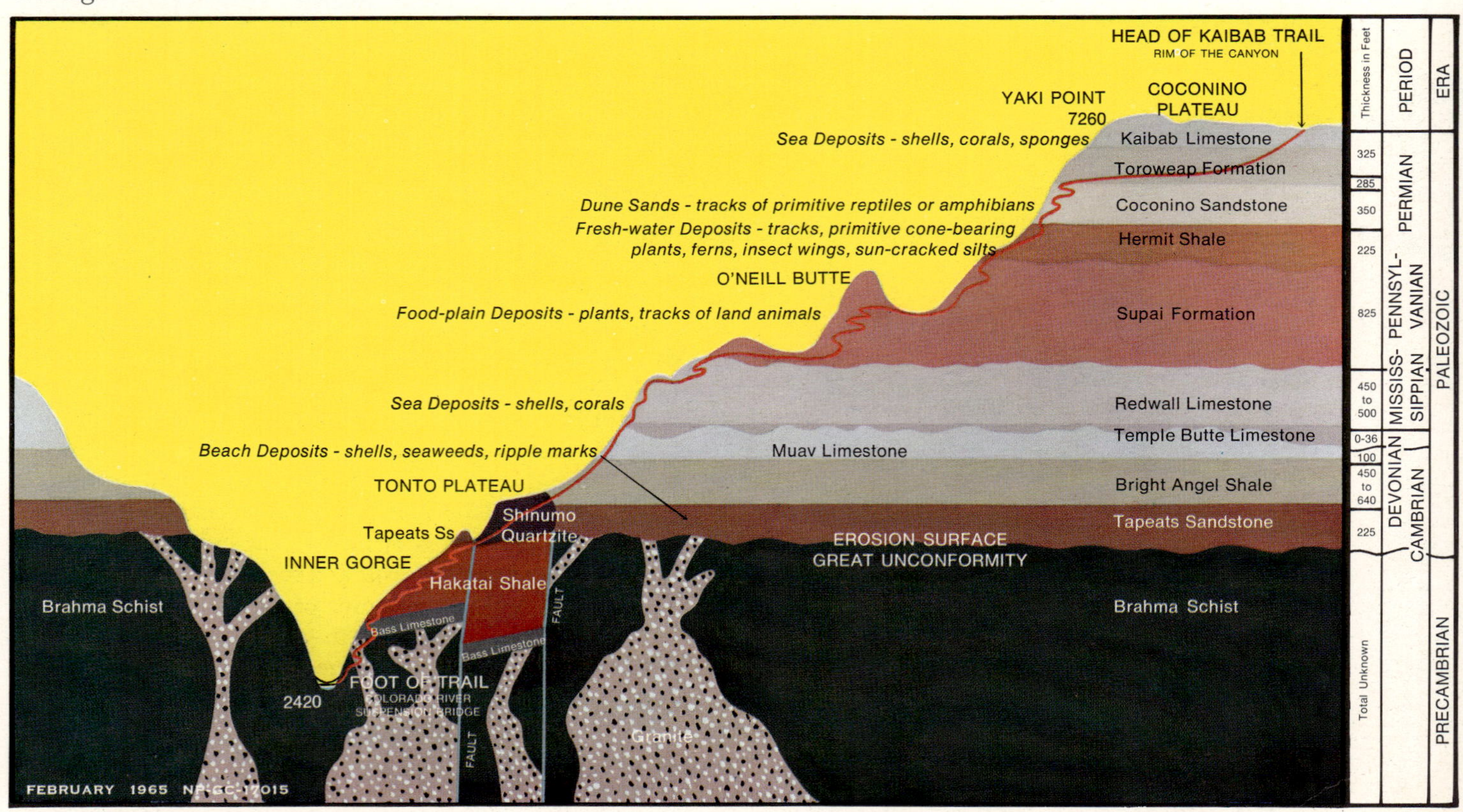

answered. "And I can't see any quartz crystals. I can scratch it with my glass, so it's one of the soft rocks."

Bill rubbed some water on the rock and smelled it. "It doesn't have an earthy smell or feel muddy, so it's not shale. Now for the vinegar test."

O'Neill Butte (6072 feet), which are marked with their top elevations, were located on the map.

Then Mr. Baker passed out to each student a card on which was typed the name of a rock formation and the altitude at which it would be found.

"Sing out when you think you have found the formation named on your card. Then we'll look for a typical rock to test and photograph. You have the colored cross section in your notebook to give you the color you'll be looking for. You'll each keep a check list for each rock formation we find. If you miss something, you can check with the secretaries who will be keeping notes for our school exhibit. Kirk has an altimeter and will give us the elevations."

After Mr. Baker explained the rules for hikes in the Canyon and Jack took a group photograph, he dropped back with Mr. and Mrs. Martin to watch the class start examining the rock exposed in the wall where the top of the trail had been cut.

Isabell Lopez was busy studying her card and the cross section in her notebook.

"What's the altitude, Kirk?" she called.

Kirk read the altimeter and called back, "A cool 7200 feet above sea level."

"Hmmm, that fits," Isabell was saying. "And I'd say the color was light gray. Any you boys found a good specimen yet?"

"This looks like one," Worden Mills answered. The group gathered around a flat piece of rock about 4 by 6 inches.

"My card says 'Kaibab Limestone,'" Isabell said. "The altitude is right, the color is right. Is it limestone?"

Allan Taylor ran the test for limestone. Soon after the vinegar hit the surface, little bubbles formed.

"Our first find!" Jan shouted. "And it's a sedimentary rock."

Jan was the secretary who would keep notes on the sedimentary rocks which the Rockhounds would find — the shales, sandstones, and limestones which had been formed from particles of older rocks squeezed together by pressure and chemically cemented. So she filled in the notes for the Kaibab Formation while the others wrote in their notebooks. Jack laid the rock on a dark cardboard for contrast and took its picture. Then he dictated the photographic notes to Betty Ball, who was acting as his secretary.

Down the trail, the gray-buff rock was identified as Larry Klein's Toroweap Limestone, and another formation was recorded in Jan's notebook. Things were happening fast and furiously.

Coach Martin, who had been moving down the trail at an easy pace and watching the fun, found a log put across the trail to keep it from washing out during a storm.

"Looks like a take-off board for a broad jump," he said. "But just look at that pit!"

"Better wear a parachute, Coach," Joe Heck advised.

Bill Smith had been watching for his formation to show up and so didn't miss the thin sandy layer in the wall and the beginning of a new buff rock. A nice-size specimen was soon found, and the group gathered around Charley Case while he examined it with a magnifying glass.

"It's made up of grains of sand," he reported.

And then everyone had a look at the specimen through the magnifying glass.

"It looks like my Coconino Sandstone," Bill Smith de-

Coconino sandstone wall beside the trail

clared. The rest agreed with him. Checking her notes after writing down the altitude, Ruth reported that they were already 1,000 feet below the rim.

Mr. Baker pointed out the cross-grain markings of the Coconino Sandstone layer. Looking across the Canyon, the group could see a similar layer just below the North Rim and also near the top of many of the formations in the Canyon itself. A hard layer like the Coconino does not erode easily.

The trail here was fairly steep with hairpin turns and sharp dropoffs on some of the switchbacks. Mrs. Martin smiled to herself when she saw she wasn't the only one hugging the inside of the trail. It was a little scary, but that was part of the fun.

Where the trail suddenly flattened out, Coach Martin pointed ahead.

"Look at the trees, kids. That must be Cedar Ridge."

Then he wandered over to where Bill and Allan were huddling over a pile of flat reddish rocks. They had been able to make a scratch with a piece of glass, but they couldn't find any quartz grains and the vinegar dropped on it did not bubble. Water rubbed on it didn't get muddy, but the rock was slippery. Bill slammed two of the rocks together and one of them cracked apart in a flat layer.

"Hermit Shale," Larry said and waved his card.

"But it's very hard," Bill replied. "And I thought it would be more like a mud rock."

"Shale should be hard. And look how it split," Manny put in.

It was agreed to record this rock as Hermit Shale, so the notes were made and the pictures taken. Kirk called out the elevation of 6,015 feet to be included in the field notes.

Amy Carter called out, "Girls, we have company." A troop of scouts carrying backpacks came swinging down the trail.

"Take it easy, fellows! You'll be fined for speeding," Coach said.

Their leader stopped a minute to tell Coach that the boys were out to earn a Boy Scout Award for hiking from Rim to River and writing a report about the trip.

Cedar Ridge was a flat area, which Coach said would make a good basketball court, and his wife kidded him about always thinking of sports.

FOSSILS AT CEDAR RIDGE

Looking around the flat area, Laura Stratton remembered that they were supposed to find a fossil exhibit. The group scattered to look, and it was Laura herself who found the Park Service exhibit with fern leaf imprints and a fossil of an insect wing in the rock. Pam and Isabell made detailed sketches of these while Jack took his photos.

"We've hiked a mile and a half, and there's two and a half more to go before lunch on Tonto Plateau. We'd better move."

The trail from the ridge down into the Natural Arch was steep, and its corkscrew course with its switchbacks could be seen far below. The Rockhounds hiked down the trail in single file.

At the bottom of the Arch, Allan Taylor picked up a reddish rock. He had found his formation — Supai Sandstone. The reddish color was from grains of hematite, one of the iron minerals. Checking his chart he found that the Supai Formation was 825 feet thick.

Joe Heck's formation was next so he led the group down the trail, with Kirk just behind calling out elevations. In short order, they were down to 5,000 feet, and Joe held up a sample from a new formation. Art went to work with his test and the rock proved to be limestone. But the color was blue-gray instead of red. Joe checked the description for the Redwall Limestone — "red-stained, light-gray limestone."

Bill Smith remembered he had read that the red stain came from iron minerals washed down from above and that this 500-foot layer was composed of a very pure gray limestone. They had found an unstained piece. A special note of this was made in the field notes. Mr. Baker asked Jack to take a photo of a red specimen, too, because this layer is called the Redwall layer of the Canyon and is an important landmark.

Art and Laura had the next two formations, and Mr. Baker knew these could be hard to find. Art's Temple Butte was purplish gray and brown, and Laura's Muav Limestone was gray mixed with a gray siltstone and only about 136 feet above Tonto Plateau.

Sharp-eyed Art quickly found a purplish limestone rock. "It isn't easy to find this formation. It comes in pockets of rock instead of a layer," he observed.

Next Laura found the Muav Limestone.

FUN AND FOSSIL FIND ON THE TONTO PLATEAU

All this talk of layers had brought thoughts of layers of ham and cheese between rye to Coach, so he and his wife went ahead to pick a spot for the picnic on the plateau.

Low bushes and prickly pear cactus grew along the trail where it flattened, and the ground was covered with gray-green rocks. Kirk picked up a flat piece, and all agreed that this was the specimen for his Bright Angel Shale. Art said that another of the iron minerals gave it the greenish color. Now they were down to 3,800 feet.

Worden Mills was scouting around off the trail when he exclaimed, "Come, look at this. It must be a trilobite." In a large greenish-gray rock he pointed out a fossil that looked like a big beetle with its ribs showing.

"You have a prize!" Mr. Baker exclaimed. "Trilobites are important in determining the age of rock formations. Trilobites of changed shape and size are found for different ages. Better draw this, Pam."

It was a good walk on fairly flat ground again after the steep descent, and the Rockhounds hurried on to join Coach and his wife. These two had taken off their knapsacks and were sitting on a rock.

"Have a rock for a seat," Mrs. Martin invited gaily. "There are no picnic tables here and no water, so enjoy your sandwiches, but go easy on the water in your canteens. It's over two miles to Phantom Ranch."

Laughing, the Rockhounds spread out to have lunch. After eating, some lay on their backs to rest, and when Tom came back from his exploring to report he had found a sign labeled Tonto Trail pointing to the west no one was interested in going that way. Coach produced a baby football from his knapsack and started a game of passing. He called to Mr. Baker that this had to be the first football game on Tonto Plateau.

It was two o'clock when Mr. Baker's whistle called them together and they started down the trail. Jan had the card

TOPOGRAPHIC MAP
BRIGHT ANGEL QUADRANGLE
TRAIL GUIDE
GN MN
15°
267 MILS
0°40'
12 MILS
UTM GRID AND 1962 MAGNETIC NORTH
DECLINATION AT CENTER OF SHEET
SCALE 1:62500
4 MILES
3000 0 3000 6000 9000 12000 15000 18000 21000 FEET
1 5 0 1 2 3 4 5 KILOMETERS
CONTOUR INTERVAL 80 FEET
DOTTED LINES REPRESENT 40-FOOT CONTOURS
DATUM IS MEAN SEA LEVEL
U.S. Geological Survey
GRAND CANYON NATIONAL PARK
Shiva Temple
Osiris Temple
Horus Temple
Tower of Set
Trinity Creek
Phantom Creek
Isis Temple
Cheops Pyramid
Dana Butte
Buddha Temple
Buddha Cloister
Hillers Butte
Clement Powell Butte
Hattan Butte
Johnson Point
Sturdevant Point
Jones Point
Haunted Canyon
The Colorado
BRIGHT ANGEL CANYON
Transept
Wall
Ribbon Fall
Sumner Butte
The Box
Phantom Ranch
Suspension Bridge
Campground
Gaging Stations
Bradley Point
Clear Creek
CLEAR CREEK TRAIL
GRANITE
Rapids
Cremation
Bright Angel Point
Grand Canyon Lodge
Powerhouse
Manzanita Point
Komo Point
Cottonwood Camp
Campground
Bright Angel Trail
N. KAIBAB TRAIL
N. KAIBAB
RIVER
RIVER TRAIL
River Resthouse
Suspension Bridge
The Tipoff
Plateau Point
Indian Gardens
Campground
Pipe Spring
Burro Spring
Pipe Creek
O'Neill Butte
Cedar Ridge
KAIBAB TRAIL
Yaki Point
Cedar Spring
Salt Creek Rapids
Granite Rapids
Horn Creek Rapids
COLORADO RIVER
TONTO TRAIL
Monument Creek
Salt Creek
Cope Butte
Cedar Spring
Hopi Point
Powell Pt Mem
Maricopa Point
The Battleship
The Alligator
Mohave Pt
Hopi Wall
Cathedral Stairs
Breezy Point
Lookout Point
Fourmile Spring
Pima Pt
The Abyss
HERMIT TRAIL
Ninetyfour Mile Creek
Ninetyone Mile Creek
BRIGHT ANGEL TRAIL
Garden Creek
Resthouse
Grandeur Point
Yavapai Pt Museum
Mather Pt
Water Tanks
Trailer Park
Visitor Center
Picnic Area
National Park Service
Training Center
Grand Canyon
Yaqui Point
TONTO TRAIL
Shiva Temple

for the Tapeats Sandstone and not far down the trail she found a brown rock. Allan's magnifying glass showed the coarse quartz grains in the hard rock which forms the top 200 to 300 feet of the cliff beneath Tonto Plateau.

The trail now looked as if it had been carved out of a rock wall, and Manny Parker was way ahead of the group when he yelled back, "Here's a piece of Shinumo Quartzite."

"No kidding," Mr. Baker yelled back.

Manny was right. Charley Case inspected the piece of purplish-brown rock and agreed with Manny that it was Shinumo Quartzite.

Jack Sharper and Manny walked ahead and Jack found a sign, "The Tipoff," around the bend. It was easy to understand the name "Tipoff" after looking down the steep drop-off to the river below. Jack took a picture of Manny on the edge. The rest of the Rockhounds caught up and had their first view of the Colorado River far below since starting the hike. There were many exclamations over the spectacular view from "Tipoff."

Now Amy Carter was in the lead looking for red rocks of the Hakatai Shale, and she was very proud of the beautiful piece she found for Jack to photograph.

THE SUSPENSION BRIDGE

Everyone was anxious to get down to the river, but only Mrs. Martin and Mr. Baker seemed to be tiring a little. Joe Heck and Coach were the first to reach the tunnel in the rock that led to the suspension bridge across the river. In his hurry Joe completely missed the new rock formation, but Tom Hardin's card read Brahma Schist and he was looking for it. The Rockhounds examined carefully the dark-gray rock Tom found. It looked like a slate but was very hard, and no grains of sand or quartz could be seen with the magnifying glass. Its up-and-down platy streak clinched its identification as the oldest rock exposed in the Canyon.

When Mr. Baker caught up he confirmed the identification and then showed them how the cables for the suspension bridge were anchored in Brahma Schist on both sides of the river.

"This bridge is 440 feet long, and those eight steel cables are 550 feet long. When the bridge was built, 42 Havasupai Indians carried the cables down the trail. For someone watching from above it must have looked like a big snake going down the trail."

"You're kidding," Worden said as he looked back up the trail.

"No, it's the truth," Mr. Baker solemnly declared.

Everyone had gathered at the tunnel before Coach would let the group start across the bridge with its high wire fence on each side of the narrow wooden footpath.

"No pushing or shoving. Just enjoy the scenery," was his caution.

There were all sorts of shrieks and shouts of laughter as the Rockhounds crossed the swaying bridge 78 feet above the river. At four o'clock the shadows were falling as the sun hid behind the rim high above, but the tips of the formations in the Canyon were shining with gold.

OVERNIGHT AT PHANTOM RANCH

At the far side of the bridge a sign pointed toward Phantom Ranch only 0.9 mile away, and the group picked up speed. Soon the cottonwood grove appeared, then the recreation building, the swimming pool, and the cabins. Coach registered the group and assigned cabins. He pointed to the showers and the pool and suggested a swim before dinner. After the trail, a swim sounded perfect, but it was only a quick dip. Coach's whistle was calling them to dress for dinner.

And what a meal! Mountains of mashed potatoes, thick slices of roast beef, vegetables, rolls, pie, and all the iced tea they could drink.

Some of the boys pitched horseshoes after dinner. Mrs.

Boy Scout Trail Awards

On the trail

The suspension bridge over the Colorado River

Martin patched up a few blisters and broke out the liniment for sore muscles. By unanimous vote, the Rockhounds decided it was early to bed and soon the lights went out in the cabins.

UP BRIGHT ANGEL TRAIL

The group departed early the next morning. They crossed the river on the foot bridge and hiked on the River Trail where Jack found a boulder of Zoroaster Granite. They continued the hike to the river house, then up Pipe Creek Canyon on the way to the top.

The climb began gradually, but soon the trail started switching back and forth. The boys were calling out formation names like professionals and pointing out the layers in the canyon wall. The Rockhounds were helping Pam look for the Bass Formation. They spotted the red-gray layer of rock above the rest house, and Larry Klein climbed up the cliff for a specimen. When the limestone test was positive Pam could say that the last layer had been found.

On up the corkscrew trail the group hiked. Just below Tonto Plateau, Mr. Baker pointed out the Great Unconformity and Bright Angel fault, which could be seen on the canyon wall across from the trail. Here the rocky layers were tilted instead of lying flat.

It was a welcome relief to reach Tonto Plateau with its fairly flat land and see the lush green bushes and cottonwood trees of Indians Gardens close ahead. Coach was encouraging some of the girls with promises of "Chow time at Indian Gardens!" and everyone picked up speed at the prospect of lunch.

Indian Gardens was a nice picnic spot with tables and running water. Sandwiches and cake were soon devoured. No football this time; resting on the grass and talking were more inviting. After a good rest the whistle brought the Rockhounds to their feet.

At each of the rest houses, named "3 mile" and "1½ mile," the group did just that — rest — while they looked back down the trail and across the Canyon at the colored layers of rocks they had walked so far to see. The final hike to the top seemed endless. Back in their cabins after dinner, the boys and girls collapsed in bed knowing they could sleep late the next morning.

When the bus left Grand Canyon the next day with Baker's Rockhounds, it headed for Tuba City, and everyone was surprised when it turned off on a desert road. Soon it stopped and Sue let out a yell when she saw the sign "Dinosaur Tracks." The bus was empty in a second, and minutes later the first big three-toed track was found. After the

track had been admired and photographed, Sue ran back to Mr. Baker to thank him for the surprise.

Mr. Baker smiled at her excitement and said, "Now, we can go home."

Laura Stratton, the quiet one, spoke up, "Thanks to Mr. Baker and Sue for this great trip."

And everybody cheered.

THINGS TO EXPLORE AT HOME

1. Find out how to calibrate an altimeter with a barometer.

2. Obtain rock specimens in your home area.

3. Classify your rock specimens as: Igneous, Sedimentary, Metamorphic.

4. Search until you find rocks which test for limestone, sandstone, shale, conglomerate.

5. Visit a rock and mineral shop.

6. Find out about stones that will make jewelry.

7. Get information and a map about the geology of your state.

8. Start a mineral collection.

9. Set up a field-note card index for your specimens.

10. Assemble a rock and mineral testing kit.

11. Learn where fossils may be found in your locality.

12. Visit a museum where minerals are displayed.

13. Obtain and study a U.S. Geological Survey topographic map of your locale from the U.S. Geological Survey, Map Information Office, Washington, D.C. 20242. Also request a descriptive folder of map symbols.

14. Write to Grand Canyon Council, Boy Scouts of America, P.O. Box 8, Flagstaff, Arizona 86001, for Trail Award requirements, or the Arizona Cactus-Pine Girl Scout Council, 1515 East Osborn Road, Phoenix, Arizona 85014, for Canyonlands Trails Award requirements.

SPECIAL NOTE. *Permit required to camp at established campgrounds on Kaibab and Bright Angel Trails and at Cottonwood and Phantom Ranch campgrounds. Write two months in advance to Superintendent, Grand Canyon National Park, Grand Canyon, Arizona 86023. Give requested dates, campground and number in party.*

Fossil dinosaur track

CREATION OF THE COLORADO RIVER AND GRAND CANYON

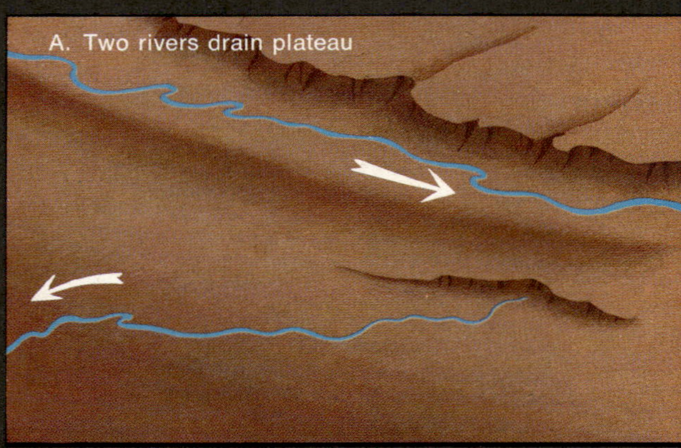

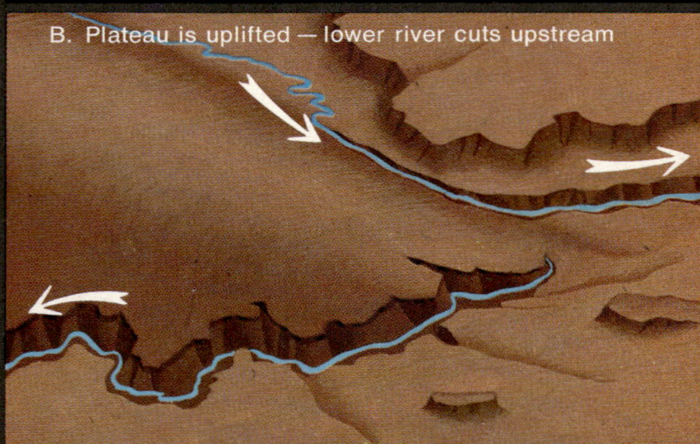

I OLDER PRECAMBRIAN ERA (2 billion — 1500 million years ago). Mountains were pushed upward by forces in the earth's crust, and hard rocks, called schist and granite, were formed. During millions of years, these mountains were worn down by weathering and washed away. Today, remnants of these mountains and rocks are at the bottom of the Canyon where the Colorado River flows.

No fossils are found in these rocks.

II YOUNGER PRECAMBRIAN ERA (1500 — 600 million years ago). Changing seas covered the flattened mountains and left sediments which formed layers of mudstone, shale, pebble conglomerate, organic limestone, and sand-grained quartz many thousand feet thick. Later, the formation of fault-block mountains broke and tilted these layers. A long period of erosion left only remnants of these layers in the eastern Grand Canyon.

Indirect fossil evidence of primitive algal life is found here.

III PALEOZOIC AREA (600 — 230 million years ago). Layers of sandstone, shale, and limestone were formed when seas and rivers again overflowed the region many times and left sediments. These rock deposits make up the upper two-thirds of the Canyon walls.

Trilobite

Fossils are found in each of these nine layers. Fossils of shells, armored fish, and trilobites are abundant. Imprints of ferns, conifers, and insect wings have frequently been found, and tracks made by four-footed amphibians and reptiles are not uncommon.

Dinosaur

IV MESOZOIC ERA (230 — 63 million years ago). A series of layers of sedimentary rock accumulated 4,000 to 8,000 feet above today's Canyon rim level. Erosion has worn this away in this area except at Cedar Mountain east of Desert View, Red Butte on the road to Williams, and at the Painted Desert. There is also a layer of hard red sandstone and shale containing fossil dinosaur footprints at nearby Tuba City.

Can you imagine dinosaurs that weighed tons and were 40 feet long roaming around here! This was the Age of Dinosaurs, but these animals became extinct, perhaps because climate and surroundings changed faster than they could adapt.

V CENOZOIC ERA (63 million years ago to the present). We now are living in Chapter V. This is the Age of Mammals. The land form has again changed. Volcanos have erupted. Formations of Chapter IV were removed by erosion, and a flat plateau developed over much of this area. This set the stage for the formation of Grand Canyon.

*A student naturalist
tells the geologic history
of the Canyon area
and how the Canyon
was formed*

Hear How It Happened

In the museum and auditorium overlooking the Canyon at Yavapai Point people were studying the fossils, rocks, models of the Canyon, and looking at Canyon features through binoculars.

An attractive girl with a National Park Service insignia on her sleeve moved to the front of the room and spoke into the microphone.

"Please be seated and I will tell you how the Canyon was formed. I am a seasonal naturalist on the Ranger's staff.

"When you look into Grand Canyon you are viewing an instant replay of two billion years of earth-forming events in this region. Shells, leaves, footprints, and other things are found as fossils in the rock formations. These fossils help us to learn about the life forms of the different ages.

"Perhaps the best way to tell how Grand Canyon happened is to begin by explaining how the rocky canyon walls were formed layer upon layer. It is a geological story with five chapters." (An illustration makes it easier to understand; opposite page.)

HOW THE CANYON BEGAN

"About 35 million years ago a great plateau in this area was drained by two rivers. One carried water from the north to the south on the eastern side of the plateau. The other drained water from the southwestern side. A great uplift of the plateau took place and the western river rapidly started to drain the high ground to the north and by erosion of its headwaters cut back to the other river. The two rivers joined to make a mighty river that carried drainage from all directions toward the southwest. This was the beginning of the present Colorado River, which has for the past 10 million years been carrying away rock and soil to sculpture the Grand Canyon.

"The grinding force of sand and rock is tremendous. Soft limestone and sandstone layers of the Canyon wore down rapidly and undermined layers of shale as the river cut through uplifted Chapter III rocks. The harder layers of rock stand as cliffs protecting the weaker rocks beneath them and also remain as the fabulous towers and temples with terraces. When the river reached the very hard rock of Chapters I and II, it was forced to narrow its course and slowly cut the inner granite gorge. At times volcanic activity poured lava into the river bed, but the river cut through it and kept right on rolling along.

THE CANYON CONTINUES TO FORM

"Weathering of the Canyon walls by storms, freeze and thaw, prying roots, and wind, loosens soil and rock which are carried to the river by side streams. Every day the Colorado River continues to carry away thousands of tons of silt, sand, and rock particles to slowly change the face of the Canyon. These amazing facts may help you understand the formation of Grand Canyon and why it is one of the natural wonders of the world."

*A high-adventure hike
to an Indian wonderland.
Ranger tips on survival*

see Havasu Falls

Havasu Falls is one of the most beautiful sights of the entire world. This waterfall is in the deep canyon homeland of the Havasupai Indians. A great adventure is to hike or ride horseback 11 miles down the steep trail to their blue-green waterfalls. It is about 161 miles by road from Grand Canyon Village to Hualapai Hilltop where the trail begins. It is reached by going north for 63 miles on a dirt road which turns off from Route 66 seven miles east of Peach Springs.

For now, let's join the Camp Pine Trailblazers on a grand hike to Havasu Falls.

It was late afternoon when the Trailblazers' bus arrived at Hualapai Hilltop at the start of the trail going down into Havasu Canyon.

"Shall we start down or make camp here on the rim?" Chuck Walters, the club leader, asked looking around.

Jack Hanson spoke up, "After that big meal an hour ago, I'm for hitting the trail."

No vote was needed. Everyone was eager to start the adventure, a visit to the famous Havasupai Indian Reservation with its beautiful blue-green Havasu Creek and three magnificent waterfalls.

All members of this hiking club had camping experience and some had been mountain climbing. Each carried a complete pack including a light bedroll and a canteen of water. All looked quite competent to handle any adventure that came their way.

Chuck Walters had been down the trail a dozen times. When he warned them it would be dark before they could reach the night's campsite, some of the girls worried that they would miss seeing some of the scenery.

"We'll see anything we miss coming out. Wait until you see the full moon shining on the canyon formations. That's a sight you'll never forget. Besides, it's going to be a lot cooler tonight."

So, with a heave ho, everyone swung his pack into place, and Joe Morales led off down the trail. Joe had been so quiet on the bus that Mary Edelston had asked him if he was sick.

"Not really," he replied. "Just tired, I guess." He had worked overtime as a carryout boy at the market to earn money for the trip. Joe had been to Havasu Falls two years before and wanted to visit it again. In fact, he had been the one who had talked the club into the trip. Joe was carrying an extra heavy pack because, as he put it, "Food is one of the most beautiful things in the world."

Amy Smith was the skinniest girl in the club, but she was the quickest on the trail and she followed Joe. Because he knew the trail, Chuck came next. Jane Haley, the physical ed counselor in charge of the girls, was the last in the line of sixteen as it snaked its way down the switchbacks between the rocky walls.

Joe spotted a mule deer on the rim above. Without saying anything he made pointing gestures so the rest could see it.

Sentinel rocks watch over a boy and his horse

FROM HILLTOP TO HAVASUPAI CANYON

The tricky descent of over a thousand feet to the bottom of Hualapai Canyon below the hilltop was reached before Chuck called for a rest break. The hikers were quick to reach for their canteens. The heat still radiating from the stony walls had made the hikers hot and thirsty. Packs slid off their backs as full advantage was taken of the 10 minutes which was all Chuck ever allowed for a rest break. There would be no time for exploring, but when Jenny Cappo came running from behind some bushes growing on the sandy slope shouting, "Come over here! I've found mountain lion tracks!" everyone hurried over to see.

"They sure are," Jack Kiddle, the wildlife specialist confirmed. "He must have chased a deer down here. Lions don't often leave the tree zone on the rim. These tracks are old and heading down."

"Just what we need," a couple of girls added.

As packs were shouldered, Chuck laid out the hiking plan.

"We've covered about three miles and it's five to go to the Indian village of Supai. Then three more to camp below Havasu Falls. The next two miles will follow a dry stream bed so we can make good time. Then we reach the Ladder, which is the next steep decline. At the bottom of the Ladder we enter Havasu Canyon and will follow the creek to the village. After we leave the village it will be pitch dark and we'll need our flashlights until the moon is high enough to shine into the canyon."

"Sounds scary, but fun," Alice Howe just had to put in.

"Forget being scared," Pete Jones laughed.

"How about the mountain lion?" Alice fired back.

"We'll eat him if we catch him," Pete joked.

Jane Haley started up their favorite trail song, and all joined in as they hit the Trailblazers' stride along the flat, sandy path.

The climb down the trail called "The Ladder" was tricky and slow. Suddenly, there was a big noise, and a small rock slide came tumbling past. Harry Billings, the big rockhound, had wandered off the trail to look at rock and had slipped on the shale. He had slid about 10 feet before he managed to grab a juniper tree. Luckily, no one had been hit by the rolling rocks. When the dust cleared the group turned to watch Harry examine the tear in his pants. He looked plenty mad at himself for pulling such a fool trick. They all started watching their steps more closely. Just climbing down The Ladder was thrill enough.

20

At the bottom there was a sweet smell of growing things and a little trickling sound of water.

"Havasupai Canyon," Chuck announced. "We're near the beginning of Havasu Creek. Listen to it whisper as it flows over the rocks!"

"O.K. for a rest stop, Chuck?" Joe called.

"Sure," Chuck agreed.

Again the hikers unshouldered their packs. Jane and Chuck, the two leaders, called a conference while everyone rested.

"Shall we camp here for the night or go on?" Jane asked.

"Everyone here has hiked 15 miles in a day many times. Let's go the full way," Suzy Heal spoke out. There were nods of agreement all around the circle. And it was decided to go on.

HAVASU CREEK

The trail turned into the deep canyon and it was only a short walk before they reached the creek. Starting from a spring fed by an endless supply of underground water, it widens in a short distance into a shallow creek. Minerals dissolved in the water give it the blue-green color for which it is famous. On both sides are green fields and patches of willow and cottonwood.

Margaret Hale was the first to spot a Havasupai Indian dwelling. It was built of willow branches in the shape of a cone, and smoke was coming out of the top. Chuck told them this "hawa" belonged to an old man. Some of the houses have straight sides and mud-and-brush roofs. A few Bureau of Indian Affairs prefab houses have been flown in by helicopter and set up. Further on the Trailblazers saw a boy sawing wood near his home and they stopped to talk to him and his sister.

Darkness seemed to be rushing down the canyon as they resumed hiking. More houses appeared and half a dozen barking dogs greeted them. In a few minutes they were at the village with its store, the tourist headquarters office, school, church, and new and old guest lodges, and a few small wooden houses.

Following the trail leading out of the village the hikers passed families cooking dinner outside their houses. Joe Morales was the last in line, and even the delicious odor of stew and beans did nothing to cheer up the food-loving Joe. He was dog-tired.

HIKING IN THE DARK

It was pitch dark where the trail went through the tall willows and cottonwoods. The hikers could hear the rushing of Havasu Creek as it tumbled down over little dams into rapids. Hiking in the dark slowed the pace and everyone was quiet. Jane Haley dropped back to the end of the line to talk to Joe. Suddenly there was a loud crash in the brush behind them and a wild coughing bark. Everyone froze. Jane swung around and threw the beam of her flashlight back and forth across the trail. Then she and Joe started laughing. There in the light stood a small burro with its head high in the air trying to bray. He had been asleep and the group scared him. But not as much as he had scared them.

"Caesar's ghost!" Peter exclaimed. "I thought the mountain lion had Jenny Cappo."

"I'm still shaking," Jenny confessed.

Joe Morales called for a rest break about a mile farther down the trail. They were in a clearing within earshot of Navajo Falls.

"Chuck," Joe said sitting by his pack. "I'll never make it tonight. Why don't the rest of you go on and let me bed down here? I'll hike the rest of the way and meet you in the morning."

Pete volunteered to stay with Joe, and Jane and Chuck agreed to the plan after a conference.

One of the girls started singing "I've been working on the railroad," as the Trailblazers left Joe and Pete unrolling their bedrolls. Within a few hundred yards the trail entered a clearing just as the full moon crept over the rim and the moonlight crawled down the canyon wall like a big searchlight.

Navajo Falls is beautiful by sun or moonlight

"Isn't that beautiful!" Amy exclaimed. "It's almost as bright as day."

"We're in luck," Chuck said. "The trickiest part of the hike is just beginning."

The trail began to narrow and become steep and rocky. A couple of the boys said they were going back to Joe and Pete.

"Not tonight!" Chuck retorted.

Jane Haley, who was up in front, called back, "Here it is! It's unbelievable."

Everyone hurried to catch up. The moon glow was shining on the 75-foot cascade of Navajo Falls. It looked like a million diamonds flashing.

"Positively beautiful," quiet little Helen Jones exclaimed.

After much oohing and ahing, Chuck suggested they move on. The trail again descended into the thicket of willows close to the creek, and the moonlight filtered through on the dancing ripples. Then the trail led through a little opening and directly down to the creek.

CROSSING THE CREEK

"Goodnight! Is that the foot bridge?" Jane squealed, pointing to two logs crossing the creek. The logs were about a foot apart and had little slats nailed on top like a ladder to hold them together and to act as foot steps.

"I'm afraid it is," Chuck assured her. And in a jiffy he had his climbing rope tied to a tree and was stepping across the bridge with the flashlights focused about him. On the other side he tied the rope to another tree.

"It's easy," he called back. "Come over one at a time and hang onto the rope. If you slip, let your pack go and hang onto the rope. We'll pull you out."

After a lot of squealing and a few close calls, everyone made it across safely. The evening was fresh and cool, and the pace picked up even though it was uphill again. In just a few hundred yards Chuck called back, "Get ready for the big surprise!"

The trail headed straight for the canyon wall, which was shining in the moonlight, then went down through a notch like a pass. Jack Hanson was in the lead and he let out a yell, "Look at this!"

HAVASU FALLS BY MOONLIGHT

The Trailblazers gathered on the steep narrow trail. What they saw from less than 50 yards was Havasu Creek falling as the mighty Havasu Waterfalls, 125 feet down into the travertine pools below. It was an absolute fairyland in the moonlight.

"Few people have ever seen this marvelous sight by moonlight," Chuck said. "Let's go slow and enjoy it."

Everyone was delighted. And they were happy too when they found their campsite in another 10 minutes. A quick meal of hot dogs and chocolate was devoured, bedrolls unrolled, and 14 weary hikers were asleep.

JOE AND PETE HAVE A SCARE

Daylight awakened Joe and Pete. They washed in the creek, shouldered their packs, and hit the trail.

Joe was puzzling over the trail when a big gray animal came running up behind them. Both boys spun around in fright.

"It's a coyote!" Joe yelled.

Pete started to laugh. "Never saw a coyote with a dog collar and a name tag."

"What a relief," Joe sighed as the tan police dog bounded up to him and wagged his tail. "The tag has his name on it. 'Ginger Snap'."

Ginger Snap walked a little ahead of the boys and looked

Ginger Snap knows the way

Rangers explain Canyon ecology

back over his shoulder as if asking them to follow him. Joe and Pete started after him and found the tracks left by their friends. Ginger Snap continued to lead them over the new trail until it joined again with the regular trail.

"Pretty cool having an Indian guide dog," Pete declared.

Ginger Snap seemed to enjoy the company and stayed with the boys down past Navajo Falls and to the foot bridge. After much careful balancing Joe and Pete crossed the creek on the bridge, but Ginger Snap found it easier to swim the blue-green waters. In a few minutes they were beside Havasu Falls. For these two who had missed seeing its beauty in the moonlight, the falls put on a different show. Far below where the water plunged into the pool, the spray rose catching the sunlight and breaking it into a rainbow.

Ginger Snap led the boys down the trail. Pete suddenly spotted half a dozen Trailblazers in for a morning dip in the pool under the falls.

"Hi, down there!" Joe shouted. And as the Trailblazers called back and the echoes from the canyon walls sounded out, Ginger Snap joined in the fun with happy barks.

Later at breakfast, Joe and Pete told about the rainbow they had seen in the mist of Havasu Falls, and Jane described the glittering diamonds of moonlit Navajo Falls.

Listening to the glowing descriptions, Chuck wryly remarked, "And we'll all be telling our grandchildren about this exciting hike into the Shangri La of the friendly Havasupai Indians."

This chatter was interrupted by the sound of horse's hoofs thudding on the sand. A cheerful voice said, "Your hot chocolate smells delicious." It was the Park Ranger for the Havasu Unit.

Chuck said, "Hi! This is a surprise. You're Ranger Jones. I heard you give a campfire talk on survival one time at the Grand Canyon Village. How about a repeat performance?"

"After chocolate?" the Ranger said smiling as he sat down on a log. Jane handed him a cup of steaming chocolate and thought he looked like a movie actor with his suntanned face, the good-looking uniform, and the famous ranger hat. The word was passed around, and the group took places around the Ranger.

"Thanks," said the Ranger. "It tastes as good as it smells.

I just rode down from the village on a routine check. I've never told a breakfast campfire story before but here goes for a quickie."

THE PARK RANGER TELLS HOW TO SURVIVE

"You young people are camping in one of the most fertile areas in Grand Canyon. The Indians have lived here for centuries. Now they grow good crops and have figs and

Great fun jumping into Havasu Creek

peaches. Water is good and plentiful. Survival is not a problem here except in winter, but suppose any one of you were lost on the desert up above. What should you do to survive?

"First, you need to know how to conserve the fluids of your body and to find moisture or water to keep you alive.

1. Keep your shirt or blouse on to minimize perspiration loss.

2. Likely places to find water are seeps at the bottom of rocky hills; a hole dug in the far bend of a dry river may reach damp sand and water; a clump of any vegetation may indicate ground water for roots; birds seek water and may supply a clue.

3. If you have a piece of plastic, dig a hole in the sand at a low spot and cover it with the plastic. If there is moisture in the earth, the sun's heat will condense it on the undersurface of the plastic. These precious drops will be welcome.

"Secondly, seek nourishment. There are a surprising number of things found on the desert that may be eaten if you must to keep alive. Many provide moisture as well as food. These include:

1. Cacti. *Prickly pear* stems are rich in water. The fruit is prepared by cutting off the top and peeling back the spiny skin. Then eat seeds and the moist pulp. The pancake-shaped leaves can be peeled and chewed, too. *Barrel cactus*

can be opened by cutting off the top. Pound the center into a watery pulp and dip out the mixture which is wet and bitter. The growing center stalk of the *agave* is tender and full of moisture. The pointed leaves ooze moisture when cut. The blossoms and fresh seed pods of the low-growing *Datil yucca* may be chewed and eaten. The stalk may also be chewed for moisture.

2. Edible plants include the bulb of the *wild onion* and the potatolike root of the *Sego lily* or *Mariposa lily*. Only the stem tips of the *wild gourd* are eaten — the gourd itself is a purgative. *Wild fern* may be eaten like lettuce and is often a clue to moisture. *Purslane* may be eaten as a salad green. *Seeds* and *nuts* of all kinds are nourishing. *Jimson weed* is poisonous.

3. Meat on the hoof. If it moves, eat it. Lizard and snake meat can be broiled. Tortoise, rabbit, gopher or squirrel would be a treat. A rock is a good weapon.

"Finally, being lost means you have no idea of a way to safety, so don't wear yourself out trying.

1. Seek shade and stay put. Trackers will find you faster.

2. Make three big circles in the sand for search planes to spot. Shine signals with a mirror or shiny metal.

3. If you can build a fire — smother it by day to make a smoke signal and make it blaze at night.

4. Keep confident and don't panic. Indians can live off the land and so can you.

"Survival is keeping alive. Animals, birds, trees, bushes — everything that is wild in nature — has to find a way to survive. Nature has a way of balancing survival so that the strong live and the weak pass away. This plan has been going on for millions of years, and it works very well unless man upsets the scheme.

"We Ranger-Naturalists are at your service to tell you anything we can about the Canyon, its trails, birds, flowers, trees, animals, insects — you name it and it will be our pleasure to help you."

Jane Haley jumped up and called for a long "Rah! Ranger!" cheer, and the Trailblazers gave a great cheer as Ranger Jones mounted his horse to ride up the trail.

Joe Morales looked over at Amy. "How about broiled lizard for lunch?" and ducked the boot she tossed at him.

"O.K., group," Chuck said. "As soon as we clean up camp, we head for the monkey vine swing and more fun and adventure at Havasu Creek and a hike to Mooney Falls."

EXPLORE WITH CAUTION

Tips to avoid becoming lost, thirsty, and hungry:

1. Always tell someone where you are planning to go and when you will return.
2. Always carry a compass, matches in a waterproof container, a mirror, and a police whistle.
3. Take enough food and water for your hike or trip.
4. Carry a "topo" map of the area.
5. Study the landmarks as you hike so that you can orient them to your map.
6. For safety, hike with a companion.

SPECIAL NOTE. *For information regarding indoor accommodations, guides, and horses, write the Tourist Agent, Supai, Arizona 86435. For camping permit information within the Grand Canyon National Park, write Superintendent, Grand Canyon National Park, Grand Canyon, Arizona 86023.*

*An exciting
Grand Canyon expedition
by airplane, river raft,
and muleback*

shoot the River Rapids

A small plane carrying the Brand family landed at Marble Canyon airstrip after an exciting flight above Grand Canyon from the Village. Mr. and Mrs. Brand, Bill, Alice and Helen, came from New York City to raft down the Colorado River rapids.

They were met by a station wagon and hurried to the boat landing at Lees Ferry where other people had arrived by auto. Boatmen were loading supplies and duffel on the inflated plastic rafts and lashing them in place with ropes.

Bill Brand quickly made friends with Jack, their boatman, and was climbing on and off the raft. Just as Alice and Helen ran up to the raft to ask when they would start, Carl, the chief boatman, called out, "We're ready. Everybody grab a life jacket from this pile and put it on and keep it on at all times while on the raft."

Everybody struggled into the new outfit, and then there was much laughter at the comical sight. Then Carl told everyone to take a tin cup and a holder containing knife, fork and spoon.

"Take care of your eating irons and drinking cups for the trip," he cautioned. "Now, all aboard."

It was quite a scramble. The rounded sides of the inflated rafts were about three feet high. Mrs. Brand crawled aboard on her hands and knees, while her husband boosted the two girls over the side. Bill, of course, needed no help. Dad then helped Mrs. Brand to the cross-bar plank seat in the back of the raft and told Alice to sit with her. He sat on the plank in front of the center luggage with Helen on one side and Bill on the other. He strapped the waterproof war-surplus ammunition box in which he had his camera, film and river map to the plank seat. Helen and Alice had plastic bags to keep their cameras dry.

Two college girls were already standing on the bottom of the boat in front, and the last member of the party, a young doctor, joined Mrs. Brand and Alice in the back. Jack started the outboard motor, and the rivermen on shore cast in the rope and pushed the raft out into the river. The people on shore waved goodby as the outboard motor pushed the raft out into the river where it was picked up by the current. The Brand family were off on their river run!

START FROM LEES FERRY

In a few minutes the raft ran through some ripples of rough water and there were squeals from the two college girls who were now sitting astraddle the sausagelike walls.

"That was nothing," Jack said. "In a few miles we will hit our first rapids. And you girls had better get your legs inside the raft and hang onto the guard rope."

"That was great!" Bill yelled. "When's the next one?"

"Badger Creek Rapids is our first major rapids," Jack replied. "It's five miles down."

The boat party had just begun to relax when Alice called out, "There's Navajo Bridge ahead."

It seemed strange to see this 467 foot high bridge from the river

Navajo Bridge towers above the Colorado River

after having flown over it only a few hours earlier. Bill pointed out people standing at lookouts high above.

Dad joked, "Anyone who wants to go home had better get off here."

For several miles the boats chugged along quietly and the heat of the sun became intense. Dad and the girls found many interesting scenes to photograph.

Jack broke up the fun. "Get ready for Badger Creek Rapids!" The coeds grabbed the guard rope and Dad had just time to stow his camera in the ammo box before Jack yelled again, "Hang on, everybody!"

THE FIRST RAPIDS

The raft lurched forward and seemed to go down sideways with water pouring over the side. Big boulders towered overhead. As the raft went down it bent in the middle and the outboard motor roared as it was lifted free of the water. The excitement was soon over.

Jack called up front, "How's everybody doing?"

"O.K., but wet," came the reply.

"Dr. Simpson," Jack said to the young doctor sitting with Mrs. Brand and Alice, "will you take this bucket up front and bail out some of the water we shipped going through that one?"

This gave the doctor the chance to get acquainted with the two coeds who pitched in to help him bail.

"I'm Shelley," the blonde said, "and my friend is Kim."

"And I'm Mike Simpson," the doctor replied. "How'd you like that 15-foot drop down the rapids?"

"Great!" Shelley said enthusiastically.

"Wonderful!" added Kim. "Do you know all about the rapids?"

"Not really," Dr. Simpson confessed. "Only what I have learned from my guidebook. It tells all about them."

Jack's warning call to get ready for Soap Creek Rapids interrupted their conversation. What a dive and dip this turned out to be! And much deeper than Badger. Mrs. Brand and Alice looked like wet rats, but they were both laughing as the raft reached smooth water again.

"My, I feel nice and cool now," Mrs. Brand exclaimed.

Dr. Simpson got out his guidebook. "We dropped 18 feet that time," he said.

Mr. Brand pointed ahead at the canyon walls. "We sure are digging deeper and deeper the way the walls are getting higher and higher."

"It says in here that the river drops a total of 1,913 feet between Lees Ferry and Lake Mead," Dr. Simpson added.

"Hang on again!" Jack shouted.

Sheer Wall Rapids is a tricky one, and the way the boat is steered into the rapids determines whether the run will be easy or rough. Once into a major rapids the raft cannot be steered.

Bill had been so busy going through the rapids and watching the canyon walls that he had been unusually quiet, but now he came out with an important question. "When do we eat?" he yelled back at Jack.

Over the general laughter, Jack yelled back, "Carl will land us on a sand bar opposite Hot Na Na Wash soon."

Sure enough, up ahead Carl's boat was slowing down. All four boats were beached and everyone scrambled up on the bar. The boatmen unloaded some boxes and quickly set out a buffet lunch with sliced bread, meat, cheese, pickles, and a can of mixed nuts. And there was a bucket of halozone-treated river water flavored with grape. The group lined up glad for the bite. Only Alice complained.

"Where's the peanut butter?"

"Coming up." Chief Carl reached down into a box and set it out.

After lunch the river runners began to feel like veterans as the rafts went through many rapids. At Twenty-one Mile Rapids Jack pulled his boat into some still water so the passengers could watch the other boats come down and take pictures of the action.

A series of five rough rapids were run in the next seven miles and everyone had plenty of thrills. The three Brand youngsters were getting tired and were glad to hear Jack announce that after Twenty-nine Mile Rapids they would be making camp for the night at a beach near Vasey's Paradise.

OVERNIGHT CAMP NEAR VASEY'S PARADISE

When the rafts were landed the boatmen unloaded the duffel bags on the shore and told everyone to choose a spot to spread his bedroll for the night. Mr. Brand picked a place for the family behind some big rocks near some tamarisk trees.

While the people readied their campsites and washed off the river mud, the boatmen made a fire from driftwood and prepared a steak dinner. It was a group of hungry people that lined up for the excellent meal.

Darkness came early in the deep canyon. There was no big campfire party. Everyone was tired and ready for bed.

Getting ready at Lees Ferry

Thrills for everyone   HAROLD W. TRETBAR

Bill and Helen stayed up for awhile entertaining themselves with running the spotlights of their flashlights on the sheer wall across the river, but they were not far behind the rest of the family.

The boatmen started the breakfast fire early the next morning, and the smell of coffee brought the passengers out of their bedrolls. The boatmen were anxious to get an early start on the river, but it took quite awhile to get the bedrolls packed into the waterproof bags and all of the duffel loaded and lashed down in the boats.

Finally, all was ready and the boats swung out into the stream. Helen had a chance for some fine pictures of Vasey's Paradise where ferns and other green plants growing in the canyon wall are fed by springs and water seeping through the limestone.

REDWALL CAVERN

A mile down the river Carl ran his lead boat up on the beach in front of a huge cavern carved by the river from the soft rock of the red canyon wall. Jack said that now that the river was low, sand covered the floor of this big room. All the boats beached, and Bill, Helen and Alice ran up the bank to check out the cavern. Helen was sure that it was bigger than the auditorium back at her school.

Thirty-six Mile Rapids was the next good one. Below this the water became calm again. Here the red-stained limestone walls of the canyon rose straight up for over 500 feet. Leaning back in the boat to look up at the walls made Alice feel as if she were back in New York City with its tall buildings on each side of the street.

It was only a few miles to the next stop near Royal Arches.

BERT LOPER'S BOAT

"We'll make a landing here to visit the memorial to Bert Loper, a pioneer river runner," Jack explained. "He was 77 years old when he lost his life in an accident about 15 miles back. His friends recovered his boat and pulled it up high on the bank where it rests as his memorial."

While Helen was busy taking her pictures, Bill examined the wrecked wooden boat. "I'm sure glad we're riding in a life-raft type boat instead of a little wooden boat like Bert Loper's," he concluded.

Back on the river it was not long before Jack warned, "Get ready for President Harding Rapids!"

Up ahead the lead boat had already disappeared. Kim and Shelley screamed. Jack was steering straight at a big boulder in the middle of the river where the rapids start. While the choppy waves splashed over its occupants, the boat swept safely by the rock on the side wash.

"I thought we were goners," Kim gasped.

"You have to steer at the rock to get through the rapids here," Jack explained. "Each rapids has its own special approach."

There were only a few rapids to be run during the afternoon, and the beautiful canyon scenery was the main attraction. The rock walls changed from red to gray-green and brown. The varied shapes of the towers brought exclamations from the river runners. Jack was kept busy answering questions about the river. Bill whistled when he was told that the river was as deep as 40 feet and up to 400 feet wide.

"Jack, how do the different rapids get their names?" he asked.

"Some are named from the creeks that run down the side canyons and empty the rocks into the river. Many have been given Indian names. Some rapids are called by their mile-post locations. That's the distance downriver from Lees Ferry. Others have been given the names of river pioneers or geologic formations. Shucks," he concluded, "with over 200 rapids between Lees Ferry and Lake Mead they almost ran out of names."

27

Making camp on a quiet stretch of the river

HAROLD W. TRETBAR

Sandy beaches with tamarisk appeared more frequently. One boat stopped to load driftwood for the evening fire. The boats landed on a sandy delta where Little Nakoweap Creek empties into the river. Here a side canyon cutting into the wall of the cliff gave shelter for their campsite.

EXPLORING CLIFF DWELLING RUINS

After the duffel was unloaded and campsites chosen, Carl passed the word that there was time before dinner to explore the ruins of an Indian cliff dwelling. Dr. Simpson asked Bill, Helen and Alice if they would like to join him and the two college girls in a climb up the trail to see it.

"Go ahead," Mr. Brand said. "Your mother and I will make camp."

They had everything organized and were resting when the young people came down the trail. Alice ran over to tell them about the ruins.

"There's a row of little rooms. It's on a ledge that's like a cave in the wall of the cliff."

Hungry people were gathering around as the cooks set up the chow line. It takes only a day or two on the river to build up a ravenous appetite, and the crews of the four boats fell to on the delicious chicken roasted in iron pots.

The third day on the river started with an exciting ride through Nankoweap Rapids with its 25-foot drop in one mile. Kwagunt Rapids came next with a seven-foot drop.

At the place where the Little Colorado empties its crystal-blue water into the muddy big Colorado River, the boating expedition made another landing. Led by Dad, the Brand youngsters climbed up to examine a rock shelter built by an old prospector.

"It must have been a lonely life," Alice observed.

"Do you know," Helen put in, "we haven't seen a TV program for three days."

28

Dad laughed. "And I haven't read a newspaper either, and it's almost a relief."

"Hey, gang," Bill called. "Here are some pieces of broken Indian pottery."

"Yes, Indians lived here centuries ago," Mr. Brand said. "I understand that they still come to this place for salt which they find near here."

Carl called up that the boats were ready to shove off and the Brands hurried back down the trail. Soon their boat swung past the sand bar at the mouth of the Little Colorado.

Kim pointed ahead. "Look! The scenery is changing. The rim is so high above and we are so deep below."

"That you are, baby," Shelley cracked. "And that little bump up there looks like the watchtower at Desert View."

"You've got good eyes," Jack said. "That watchtower is 7,500 feet above sea level."

"When are we going to get some rapid action?" Bill asked.

"Lava is next with a four-foot drop, but Tanner follows with a 20-foot drop, and the next one after that will be Unkar. It drops 25 feet in only 0.3 mile," Jack answered. "How does that sound?"

"Great," Bill replied.

In the next seven miles there were thrills enough for even Bill, and Alice lost her hat. At Seventy-five Mile, after running a tame rapids, Carl led the boats to a landing on a long sandy beach. It was only early afternoon, and when Carl announced that this was both their lunch and dinner stop several people wanted to know why.

SWIMMING IN THE RIVER

Carl smiled and pointed to the river. "This is a very safe beach for swimming. And you can try out your air mattresses in those ripple rapids. This afternoon we can be beach boys and girls instead of river rats for a change."

It was a fun afternoon for the Brand youngsters. Mr. Brand blew up the air mattress and took each of them for a ride in the ripple rapids. Mrs. Brand organized the campsite and then had a chance to rest. When the sun lowered behind the steep canyon wall across the river it became pleasantly cool for the big dinner party the boatmen prepared. Shelley and Kim came in from the river bragging about the tan they had acquired.

After dinner the boatmen started a game of cards by the light of a gas lantern, but the rest of the party soon drifted to their sleeping bags tired after a day full of excitement

Magnificent Redwall Cavern

Pioneer Bert Loper's boat

and fun. At home Helen and Alice liked to talk after they crawled into their beds at night, but here they were asleep without a word.

In the middle of the night Bill woke his father by mumbling, "Put out that flashlight!"

"What's the matter, Bill?" Mr. Brand asked.

Fully awake now, Bill started to chuckle. "Look at that full moon! I woke up thinking someone had a spotlight on me."

Mrs. Brand sat up in her sleeping bag and looked across the canyon. "I'm glad you woke me up," she said. "The sky and the moonlight are heavenly beautiful. Just look at those temples and cliffs and the river in the moonlight. I'll remember this sight forever."

Alice and Helen didn't even stir.

It was all business again with the boatmen the next morning, and the passengers soon learned the reason. Just below Papago Creek, a mile downstream, Carl headed his boat in for a landing, and the rest of the boats tied up alongside.

WALK AROUND DANGEROUS HANCE RAPIDS

"Here you walk," Carl said. "This is Hance Rapids and it drops 30 feet in one-half mile. We'll take the boats through and meet you at the foot."

The boatmen took each boat through the treacherous waters. The people hiking along the shore around the big rocks and boulders watched the boats go by. Bill had asked Jack if he could ride with the boat, but after watching it stand on its nose going through he understood Jack's refusal. Helen was busy taking pictures of what she was sure must be one of the greatest action scenes in the world.

Back in the boats, everyone got a good soaking running Sockdolager Rapids two miles below Hance. Here the river runs through a deep granite gorge with black stony walls on both sides, and there was little sun to dry the wet clothes. The rafts passed the mouths of several creeks before Grapevine Rapids was announced. Grapevine drops 18 feet, and its many rocks resemble a bunch of grapes. When the river became calm below the rapids, the boats moved along at a slow pace.

"It's almost noon," Mr. Brand said, looking at his watch.

Alice had climbed to the front of the boat. "I see a bridge up ahead," she called back.

"That's the suspension bridge," Jack said. "We'll be landing after we pass under it."

The Brand family hated to see the boats land. This was the end of their 88-mile river adventure. The others in the party were continuing on for the rest of the 225 miles to Lake Mead. The river runners hiked into Phantom Ranch

A way to travel from river to rim

for lunch, a shower and swim in the clear pool. Goodbyes were said to Shelley, Kim, Dr. Simpson, and the boatmen when they left the ranch.

Mr. Brand had made reservations at Phantom Ranch, and the family slept in beds that night in the rustic log cabins. It took a lot of pounding on the door to awaken the girls next morning.

After a hearty breakfast, the three youngsters went out to watch the cowboy trail boss bring up a string of mules into the corral. The Brands were riding to the top with a party which had come down Bright Angel Trail the day before. Dad was busy getting the duffel in a pile to be loaded on a pack mule.

RIDING THE MULE PACK TRAIN TO THE TOP

Frank, the trail boss, said, "Let's go!"

Alice looked at the mules. "Which one am I going to ride?"

Frank lifted her onto the littlest mule in the corral.

Alice looked down at her mule. "I feel kind of shivery," she told Frank.

"Don't be scared," Frank reassured her. "Her name is Bessie and she's as gentle as a lamb. Now let me shorten these stirrups to fit you."

Frank seemed to know the right mule for everyone. Then he gave brief instructions to the party.

"Hold the reins lightly with one hand and the saddle horn with the other. The mules know the way without steering. When we stop to give the mules a rest they will all turn out and face the edge of the trail. Don't get scared; they won't jump off the cliff."

Frank lined up the mule train. Mrs. Brand came first, then Alice and Helen. Bill and his father followed and then the other people in the party. As the mules started up the trail, Frank called back, "It's just like riding in a rocking chair." Nearly everybody laughed.

Helen looked down at the river as the mule train passed over the swaying suspension bridge. "I feel a little sad not to be down on the river. That was fun."

Bill said, "I'm glad there's a high fence on both sides of this bridge so my mule can't decide to take a swim."

The mule train went through the rock tunnel on the other side of the bridge and headed up the steep Kaibab Trail. When the mules turned toward the edge of the cliff at the first rest stop, the Brand family was silent while the people who had come down on the mule train the day before were talking about the magnificent view. But after two more stops, Helen and Alice began to talk about the view of the river they could see in spots below.

"Sounds to me as if you girls are getting mighty brave," Bill remarked. Now everyone was enjoying the ride, even Mrs. Brand.

Finally, Bill called up to Frank, "How much longer?"

Frank said the party would top out in half an hour.

The mules clippety-clopped along at a slow easy pace, and right on schedule the trail made its final turn out into the pine forest on the top of the rim at an elevation of 7,200 feet.

Frank led the mule train through the forest to the big mule barn and corral. End of trail! Everyone dismounted and the pack mules were unloaded. Done with their day's work, the mules were turned into the big corral to roll and cool off after the climb. Alice laughed as Bessie rolled and rolled and then got up and shook herself.

"That feels just as good to her as your shower will feel to you up at the lodge," Frank said.

Station wagons from the lodge picked up the weary riders and their duffel and took them to the lodge.

Looking around at his quiet family, Dad said, "My, how quiet everyone is. However, when we get back to New York, we'll be able to talk for weeks about how we explored the Grand Canyon in four days by air, by boat, and by mule."

MAJOR RAPIDS
Lees Ferry to Phantom Ranch
(after Jones, 1962)

Mile	Name	Rating (1-11)	Drop
7.8	Badger	(7)	15'
11.2	Soap Creek	(8)	17'
20.5	North Canyon	(5)	12'
52.0	Nankoweap	(3)	25'
68.5	Tanner Canyon	(6)	20'
72.4	Unkar	(10)	25'
75.2	Seventy-five Mile	(6)	15'
76.5	Hance	(11)	30'
78.6	Sockdolager	(8)	19'
81.5	Grapevine	(10)	18'

SPECIAL NOTE. *Write to Superintendent, Grand Canyon National Park, for list of authorized river guides. Reservations for mule trip river to rim made by river guide.*

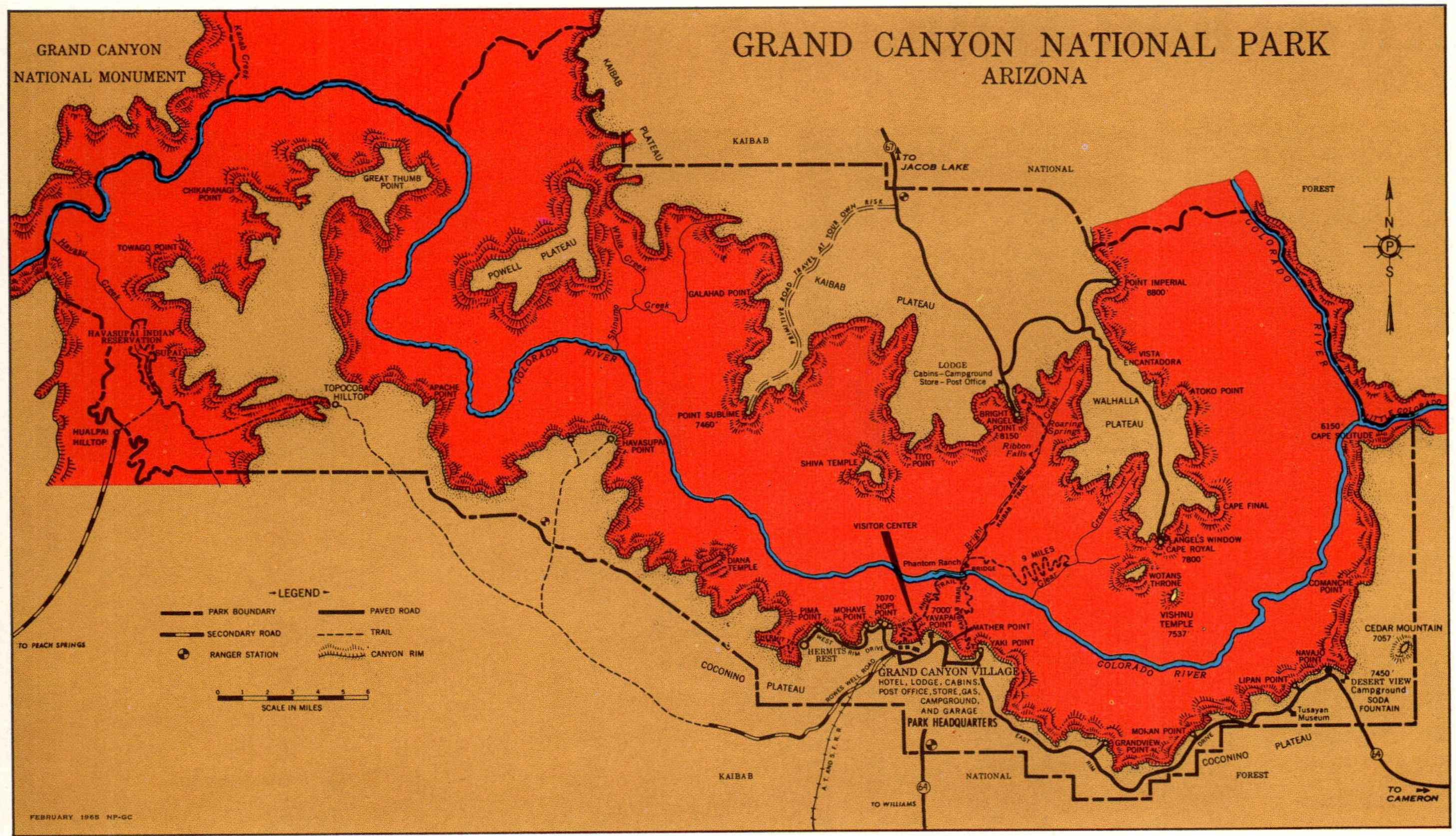

ABOUT THE AUTHOR

Become involved is the theme of Felton O. Gamble's Grand Canyon books: *Explore Grand Canyon* and *Your Grand Canyon Adventure Guide.* He writes about adventures and facts to help others have a greater appreciation of the Grand Canyon.

A former college professor and author of medical textbooks, Felton O. Gamble is a podiatrist in Tucson, Arizona. Dr. Gamble says, "It is a real joy and privilege to explore, photograph, and write about Grand Canyon."

SELECTED REFERENCES

AIM YOUR CAMERA

Grand Canyon Natural History Association and National Park Service, U. S. Department of the Interior. Nature Trail Leaflets. Available Visitor Center, Grand Canyon.

GAMBLE, FELTON O. *Your Grand Canyon Adventure Guide.* Las Vegas, Nevada: K. C. Publications, 1968.

HEAR HOW IT HAPPENED

BEAL, MERRILL D. *Grand Canyon, the Story Behind the Scenery.* Las Vegas, Nevada: K. C. Publications, 1967.

McKEE, E. D., R. F. WILSON, W. J. BREED and C. S. BREED. *Evolution of the Colorado River in Arizona.* Museum of Northern Arizona Bull.: Flagstaff, Arizona, Northland Press, 1967.

HIKE FROM RIM TO RIVER

ZIM, HERBERT S. and PAUL R. SHAFFER. *Rocks and Minerals.* New York: Golden Press, 1957.

SMITH, HUBERT A., MILO K. BLECHA, and JOHN STEINIG. *Science 4.* River Forest, Illinois: Laidlaw Bros.-Doubleday & Co., Inc., 1966.

SEE HAVASU FALLS

WAMPLER, JOSEPH. *Havasu Canyon.* Berkeley, California: Howell-North Press, 1963.

JOHNSTON, JAY and TERRY EILER. "Indian Shangri-la of the Grand Canyon." *National Geographic,* v. 137, no. 3, 1970.

SHOOT THE COLORADO RIVER RAPIDS

BELKNAP, BUZZ. *Grand Canyon River Guide.* Salt Lake City, Utah: Canyonlands Press, 1969.

SIMONS, GEORGE C. and DAVID L. GASKILL. *River Runner's Guide to the Canyons of the Green and Colorado Rivers,* 3 vols. Flagstaff, Arizona: Northland Press, 1969.

SELECTED FIELD CHECK LISTS Available at Visitor Center

Interpretive Staff, Grand Canyon National Park. *Grand Canyon Birds.* Grand Canyon Natural History Association.

Interpretive Staff, Grand Canyon National Park. *Grand Canyon Mammals.* Grand Canyon Natural History Association.

GEHLBACH, FREDERICK R. *Grand Canyon Amphibians and Reptiles.* Grand Canyon Natural History Association.

STOCKERT, JOHN W. and JOANNE W. STOCKERT. *Common Wildflowers of the Grand Canyon.* Salt Lake City, Utah: The Wheelwright Press, 1967.

TILLOTSON, M. R. and FRANK J. TAYLOR. *Grand Canyon Country,* rev. ed. Stanford, California: Stanford University Press, 1935.

ACKNOWLEDGMENTS

For their editorial assistance I am grateful to Helen R. Hauck and Kit Scheifele, Tucson, Arizona; Louise Hinchliffe, Curator/Librarian, and Jon Haman, Ranger, Grand Canyon National Park Service; and Joseph Ernst, Grand Canyon.

I wish to thank many others who have assisted in various ways: Dr. Milo K. Blecha and Dr. R. F. Wilson, University of Arizona; Dr. Dorothy Talbert, School District #1, Tucson, Arizona; Mother Abbie Tuller, Director, Tuller Schools, Tucson, Arizona; and Principal Leslie H. McQuary and Dolores Kaith of Peter Howell School, Tucson, Arizona; the students whose comments have been so helpful. Special thanks to Dr. Harold W. Tretbar for the pictures he has provided.

The willing assistance of the personnel of Grand Canyon National Park Service is acknowledged and especially that of Robert R. Lovegren, Superintendent, David Ochsner, Warren Hill, Wesley Leishman, Peter S. Bennett, Rodney Menking, and Cary Jones. Talks by Jerry Thorton, Paul Risk, and Nikki Williams have been a source of invaluable reference. Pictured in the book are Yolanda Aginiga and Jon Haman.

NASA supplied photo of Col. Frank Borman taken four hours before moonflight liftoff.

BACK COVER: *A backpacker views Havasu Falls*

Nature Field Trips
Selected Check Lists

Steller's Jay

Thistle

Chipmunk

Oak

BIRD CHECK LIST

Common on Rim Areas
White-throated Swift ☐
Red-shafted Flicker ☐
Williamson's Sapsucker ☐
Say's Phoebe ☐
Western Wood Pewee ☐
Violet-green Swallow ☐
Audubon's Warbler ☐
Black-throated Sparrow ☐
Broad-tailed Hummingbird ☐
Steller's Jay ☐
Common Raven ☐
Mountain Chickadee ☐
White-breasted Nuthatch ☐
House Finch ☐
Gray-headed Junco ☐
Pygmy Nuthatch ☐
Canyon Wren ☐
Plain Titmouse ☐
Robin ☐
Hermit Thrush ☐
Western Bluebird ☐
Western Tanager ☐
Chipping Sparrow ☐

FLOWER CHECK LIST

Rim Areas
Larkspur ☐
Creeping Mahonia ☐
Pink & White Phlox ☐
Scarlet Bugler ☐
Red Gila ☐
Goldenrod ☐
Asters ☐

Upper Inner Canyon
Primrose ☐
Wild Sweet Peas ☐
Poppy Thistle ☐
Golden Smoke ☐
Desertplume ☐
Locoweed ☐
Filaree ☐
Wild Geranium ☐
Sego Lily ☐

Lower Inner Canyon
Jimson Weed ☐
Scarlet Mallow ☐
Wild Four-o'clock ☐
Columbine ☐
Blue Larkspur ☐
Wild Mustard ☐
Milkweed ☐
White Pentstemon ☐
Nightshade ☐

MAMMAL CHECK LIST

Various Areas
Mule Deer ☐
Abert Squirrel, S. Rim ☐
Kaibab Squirrel, N. Rim ☐
Coyote ☐
Mountain Lion ☐
Ring-tailed Cat ☐
Chipmunk ☐
Rock Squirrel ☐
Gray Fox ☐
Desert Bighorn Sheep ☐
Badger ☐
Beaver ☐
Spotted Skunk ☐
Pocket Gopher ☐
Desert Wood Rat ☐

REPTILES & AMPHIBIANS

Desert Tree Toad ☐
Blue Bellied Lizard ☐
Collared Lizard ☐
Horned Lizard ☐
Desert Spiny Lizard ☐
Arizona Tree Uta ☐
Western Rattlesnake ☐
Western Striped Racer ☐
Arizona Gopher Snake ☐
Common King Snake ☐

SHRUBS AND TREES

Rim Areas
Piñon Pine ☐
Juniper ☐
Ponderosa Pine ☐
Englemann Spruce ☐
White Fir ☐
Aspen ☐
Oak ☐

Upper Inner Canyon
Box Elder ☐
Western Birch ☐
Willows ☐
Wilcox (Live) Oak ☐
Redbud (Judas Tree) ☐
Cottonwood ☐
Mormon Tea ☐
Agave (Century Plant) ☐
Yucca baccata ☐

Lower Inner Canyon
Burrowbrush ☐
Catclaw ☐
Mesquite ☐
Rabbitbrush ☐
Wild Grape ☐
Manzanita ☐
Mountain Mahogany ☐